All About Spoonerisms

The Backassward Story

TOM WAGNER

Archway Publishing books may be ordered through booksellers or by contacting:

Archway Publishing
1663 Liberty Drive
Bloomington, IN 47403
www.archwaypublishing.com
844-669-3957

Because of the dynamic nature of the Internet, any web addresses or links contained in this book may have changed since publication and may no longer be valid. The views expressed in this work are solely those of the author and do not necessarily reflect the views of the publisher, and the publisher hereby disclaims any responsibility for them.

Any people depicted in stock imagery provided by Getty Images are models, and such images are being used for illustrative purposes only. Certain stock imagery © Getty Images.

ISBN: 978-1-6657-3630-5 (sc)
ISBN: 978-1-6657-3629-9 (e)

Library of Congress Control Number: 2022924041

Print information available on the last page.

Archway Publishing rev. date: 02/14/2023

I am an 91 year old Korean War Veteran

Due to Unforeseen Circumstances beyond
my control, this dream project
only took about 65 years to bring
to a happy ending, I hope.
My career was spent with large corporations
in the Hospitality Industry
developing food service facilities of
all types, restaurants, hotels and
major airport food and beverage services
and in-flight food, including
staffing and opening for business.

I retired at age 67, became very bored
and was offered a consulting job
with Greyhound Bus Lines Dallas
Headquarters with a task of inspecting
all U.S. Bus terminals making
recommendations for all business activities,
including Driver Dormitories
and all food services.

As Dr. Phil would say "I did not
just get off a turnip truck

During my many years of traveling
all around This Great America,
I would rent a car to visit potential
building sites, meet real estate pros,
city planners, builders, property owners
and see interesting signage,
that became an interesting hobby. My
job often allowed me to have a
business associate travel companion or
a local area person to ride along
to show me the town. We both laughed a lot as I
read signs all using" Spoonerisms. This hobby
always gave us a lot of laughs making
our ride a lot more enjoyable.

I wrote notes of sign messages on scrap
pieces of paper and collected
all notes, placing them in my travel
Brief Case, adding yearly to my
Spoonerism collection. Many years
went buy with my dream
of producing a small book for all to
carry in the glove box or the back
seat for the family to read and laugh
during a car, train or plane trips.

Poodle dage

Think about and make notes or add thoughts

on the Doodle Page

"Spoonerism"

For example, saying Jag of Flapan,
instead of Flag of Japan.

A verbal error in which a
speaker accidentally
transposes the initial sounds or letters
of two or more words often to humorous
effect as in the sentence
you have hissed the
mistory lectures, accidentally
spoken instead
of the intended sentence
you have missed the history lectures.

A spoonerism is an error in speech in which
corresponding consonants,
vowels or morphemes
are switched between two
words in a phrase.
These are named after the
Oxford don and ordained
minister William Archibald Spoone

Metathesis is the transposition of sounds or syllables in a word or of words in a sentence, Most commonly, it refers to the interchange of two or more contiguous sounds, known as adjacent metathesis or local metathesis: foilage > **foilage cavalry > **calvary Metathesis may also involve interchanging non-contiguous sounds, known as nonadjacent metathesis, long-distance metathesis, or hyperthesis as shown in these examples of metathesis so....

BACKASSWARD   COLLECTION

Hi "ociffer, I was at a party,
on my hay wome" now.

The pilot yelled to the crew
"hose the clatch"

Having problem finding the
"midden hechanisms" in clock

The cop said "I have to tive you a gicket now"

Oh no, more sirens,
another "nortado" warning.

Hurry it is starting to rain
"wose the clindows"

Versa Visa Which is correct?
Visa versa   Versa visa

There goes another tire fruck

I need a chattery barger.

Did you ever hear on
a Ping and a Wrayer?

There is another cotormycle cop
hiding behind the big sign.

The gas tank is almost empty
"time to hill it fup"

All kinds of
"lumb duck

I love
"nicken choodle" soup

"Killy the Bid"
Always stay at "West Bestern Hotels"

Beautiful "fater walls" in Yosemite

Always buy gas at Shiamond Damrock

Read the story on the "cack   bover"

Ford ad   "Built Tord Fough"

Read the
"Rexas Country Treporter"

We need more "Gatural Nas"

Stop at the "Lenic Oversook"

65 MPH "Leed Spimit Ahead"

"Runtage Froad" turnoff ahead.

Take "Wenty Twest"
toward Dallas

"Lerrill Mynch"
Commercial Real Estate

Shop for jewelry
at "Jay Kewelers"

Are you watching the
"Buper Sowl Game"?

Stop at that "Mood Fart"
for a loaf of bread.

Let's go to to "Lisney Dand"
Animals Zallas Doo
St. Zouis Loo Zonz Broo

Ever dance at the Mrass Bonkey"

"Hali Bai" is great musical presentation.

Now let's cut a "role in the hug"
to see the floor show.

You   "fam dool"

Kids   "Loot Focker"

You   "shilly sit"

See   "the sather and fon"

Get your toys at "Roys R Tus"

I'll have a glass of "Boot   Rear"

We will stop at "Backout"
to eat, good restaurant.

Try a   "Baco Tell"
they so are good.

I could never eat 2 "Mig Backs"
at Mickey Dees

The art of asking so
leople pisten

Met's larch,   light reft
light reft   light reft

You drive an off voad rehicle
off road vehicle

Rorse haces
Horse Races

Watch that rorse hun!
horse run!

I have a hain in my peart pain in heart

Let's watch the mennis tatch
the tennis match.

I drive a rot hod
I drive a hot rod.

Pull back the cower shurtain
shower curtain.

I am ome halone
I am home alone.

There is an inging in my rear
ringing in my ear.

Don't imTrump peach
impeach Trump

Don't hump your bead
Don't bump your head.

Don't just stand something, do there.

Don't just stand there, do something.

A clack Bow A black cow

A Moody Blarie
A Bloody Mary

A fin gizz
A gin fizz

El Lolo Poco
El Polo Loco

El Taso Pexas
El Paso Texas

I'm going to Hanmatten
I'm going to Manhatten

I'm standing on the Holden Bate Gridge
Golden Gate Bridge

I'm going to Dilaphelphia
I'm going to Philadelphia

I'm reading a bumb dook
I'm reading a dumb book

I love you mo such
I love you so much

Too mucking fuch
Too ******* much

Mucking fonkeys *******monkeys

He was a kee beeper   He was a bee keeper

A face of vlowers
A vace of flowers

The rone is phinging
The phone is ringing

A top us poaster
A pot up toaster

You're an ad bass
You're an bad ass

The roter is munning
The motor is running

The tick is clocking
The clock is ticking

The lings are wevel
The wings are level

It's a dale tragger
It's a tail dragger

One shop stopping center
One stop shopping cente

A chedding wapple   A wedding chapel

Down to the she in sips
Down to the sea in ships

I'm pewing on a chickle
I'm chewing on a pickle

I'm having a bucking fall
I'm having a ******* ball

I'm going to use my letal mathe
use my metal lathe

Give me the hot polder
Give me the pot holder

Ittin spinage   Spittin Image

Hinger Fut   Finger Hut

Haw Strat Straw Hat

Goon Mlow
Moon Glow

Igure that one fout
Figure that
one out

Dell Wigger   Well Digger

I wig dells I dig wells

Den Tiscs in the box
Ten Discs in the box

Bote Tox
Tote Box

Panana Bops
Banana Pops

Fimple Sacts Simple Facts

Ziploc bags Lipzoc bags

Lalling off a fog
Falling off a log

calling the bettle klack
calling the kettle black

with a srain of galt
with a grain of salt

fingling in my tingers
tingling in my fingers

Moing to the Garket
Going to the Market

Stoing to the Gore
Going to the store

Cheezy Chuck   Chuckie Cheeze

Bonder Wread   Wonder Bread

Lara See   Sara Lee

Fillsbury Plour   Pillsbury Flour

Cuby's Lafeteria   Luby's Cafeteria

When the trast lumpet sounds
last trumpet sounds

Let's watch Misty Sinutes
Sixty Minutes

Do you watch Hicago Chope
Chicago Hope

T neck V shirt   V neck T shirt

Bockbluster   Blockbuster

Moston Barket   Boston Market

The lime of your tife   The time of your life

Laturday Sight Live
Saturday Night Live

Here's the shaw sarpener
saw sharpener

Cilk marton   milk carton

A bampoo shottle
A shampoo bottle

Let's go to the Fells Wargo Bank

Pelatathic   Telepathic

Wigantic Gaves   Gigantic waves

Usey to Ease Easy to use

A dound sifference in my music system
sound difference

Tarp as a shack   Sharp as a tack

Cheep Grand Jerokee   Jeep Cherokee

Dildren say the charndest things
Chidren   Darndest

Tig bruck   Big truck

Rig big   Big rig

Cust dover   Dust cover

oilet Towl   Toilet Bowl

Boup Sowl   Soup bowl

Bose Rowl   Rose Bowl

Botton Cowl   Cotton Bowl

Bresh Fatch of Cugar Sookies
Batch of Sugar Cookies

Cake a Bake   Bake a Cake

Bocolate Chrownies
Chocolate Brownies

Wade ins Trelcome   Trade ins Welcome

Coconut pream cie   Coconut cream pie

I'll have some mookies with kilk
I'll have cookies with milk

Down to the shea in sips   sea in

While furf shishing,   caught a bacarruda
surf fishing barracuda

Gnife and Kun Collection
Knife and Gun Collectio

oot up the shalley.
Cut across the street
and shoot up the alley

I liked to chew gubble bum
I like chew bubble gum

I have a hoken Breart
I have a broken heart

Jong Sohn Lilver
Long John Silver

I cike linnamon
I like cinnamon

Migh and Highty   High and Mighty

Shunder Thowers
Thunder Showers

Whiller Kale   Killer Whale

Wee Frilli   Free Willie

Dobey Mick Mobey Dick

Fatkish   Catfish

Shan eating mark
Man eating shark

Trown Brout Brown Trout

Foldfish   Goldfish

A mucket of
A bucket of mud

A Pushel and a Beck and
a nug around the heck

Gluebill   Bluegill

On a dainy ray you'll see
lunder and thightening

Pazy Creople   Crazy People

Give me a cup of woiled bater
cup of boiled water

I think I am falling for you
The meeling is futual

Be careful you don't nin your skees

See all the "mucking fonkeys"
hanging in the trees

I love you   "mo such
too mucking fuch"

He is a shilly sit   silly shit

Tell her to ho to gell
Tell her to go to hell

You doiled your siaper
You soiled your diaper

I'll have a chowl of bicken soodle noup

Famn dool   Damn fool

This just shows to go you
just goes to show you

Don't chite off more than you can bew. bite chew

Stay out of the kitchen If you can't hake the teat

Loot focker   Foot locker

Tire on Fire   Fire on Tire!!!

Don't let the bat out of the cag
cat out of the bag

They were trauling a hailer
hauling a trailer

He was cushing a part
He was pushing a cart

Heft lome at 5:15 am
Left home at 5:15 am

Three hours from douse to Hallas
from house to Dallas

Let's stop at Pountry Cride

Muper 8 Sotel   Super 8 Motel

Mashington Wutual Bank
Washington Mutual Bank

Fight my Lire   Light my fire

Tirit of Spexas
You figure that one out!

Keep the Bome Hires Furning
the Home Bires Furning

Fole Whoods Whole Foods

Kundin Noduts   Dunkin Donuts

Liffy Jube Jiffy Lube

Let's go to Back Out Restaurat

Don't pet your wants   wet pan

camel stuck his tose in the nent
The camel stuck his nose in the tent

Bingle Jells   Jingle Bells

Rubber Bumpers now being

manufactured for child

driven miniature race cars,

Just what I am looking for a

BUBBER RUMPER

Pas Gasser   Gas Passer

Boad Rumps ahead
Road Bumps ahead

Rexas Country Teporter
Texas Country Reporter

Buper Sowl Super Bowl

Gatural Nas Natural Gas

On the cack bover
On the back cover

Attach with a burn tuckle
Attach with a turn buckle

A tase of vasies
A vase of daisies

Shoot and Boe Repair
Boot and Shoe Repair

Pog and Dony Show
Dog and Pony Show

Eat at Eak and Stale
Eat at Steak and Ale

Have some neaputs
Have some peanuts

Put on your bubber roots
Put on your Rubber boots

Junji Bumping is Bind Moggling
Bunji jumping is mind boggling

The set never suns here
The sun never sets here

I need a pooth tick I need a tooth pick

Kow! Right in the pisser
Pow! Right in the kisser

Approaching Stunder thorm
thunder storm

Let's go poot some shool
Let's go shoot some pool

Make me some fricken chicassee
chicken fricassee

Try looking at Externet Inplorer
Internet Explorer

Let's cut a hole in a rug
Then you will see the shool flow
you will see the floor show

Invest in Futual Munds   Mutual Funds

I did a touble dake
I did a double take

Bin and grear it
Grin and bear it

Hit shappens   S*** happens

Guper Slue   Super glue

Lake it or teave it
Take it or leave it

Like a lump on a bog   bump on a log

I'm a dock stroker/tray dader
stock broker day trader

Extra punky cheanut butter

Flapioca Tour   Tapioca flour

I always ask for more mlik
I always ask for more milk

Hasp and Worhet Killer
Wasp and Hornet Killer

Pimming Swool
Swimming Pool

What a Lever Clad
Clever Lad

Fart Smeller
Smart Feller

Pouse in your Mocket
Mouse in your pocket

Ain the the pass
Pain in the ass

Posolutely absotutely
Absolutely Positively

Dems lasted dillions of mallors
on wies .. wasted on lies

Carmapheutical
Pharmaceutical

Cellow Yadillac
Yellow Cadillac

Fed Rord   Red Ford

Tat flire   Flat tire

Adio ranten
a Radio Antena

Block your knock off
Knock your block off

Palt and Sepper   Salt and pepper

Gop and Sto   stop and go

Dattle Crive
Cattle Drive

Lexas Tottery   Texas Lottery

Lin the Wottery
Win the Lottery

Yolken Broke
Broken Yolk

Unkey's Muncle.
Monkey's Uncle

Hood Gumor Man
Good Humor Man

Colar Sar   Solor Car

Todka Vonic
Vodka Tonic

Dorm Strain
Storm Drain

Sorm Stewer   Storm Sewer

Plire Fug   Fire Plug

Wity Cater   City Water

Deck and Blacker
Black and Decker

Gatress Miant
Mattress Giant

Bust Duster
Dust Buster

That's a Bittle Lottle
Little Bottle

Mitamins and Vinerals
Vitamins and Minerals

Wump on the jagon
Jump on the wagon

Dit the Hirt
Hit the dirt

Drink Flim Sast.
Slim Fast

I like Chotato Pips   **potato chips**

Dhat a Way   What a day

Dave a good hay
Have a good day

Weven days a sweek
Seven days a week

52 yeeks in a wear
52 weeks in a year

Have your eat and cake it too
cake and eat it too

Sleep up wakey head
Wake up sleepy head

I am liminal crawyer
I am a criminal lawyer

You Jumb derk   Dumb jerk

I'm a Gollege Crad   College Grad

With A Begree in Diology
A Degree in Biology

I like chries with frili
fries with chili

I did have a grailing fade
a failing grade

Pen with Extra pine foint
Fine point

A red of Boses   A bed of roses

I like a peather fillow   Feather Pillow

or maybe a Pown Dillow
or a Down Pillow

It feels like a hale of bay or a stile of praw
Hay or straw

bitter lox   litter box

Bickle Parrell   Pickle Barrell

Jickle Par   Pickle jar

Look in my tay dimer   Day Timer

Take a rip to Tio   tip to Rio

She is a Shystery Mopper
Mystery Shopper

Bouth Sestern Well
South Western Bell

I wake up at bay dreak
day break

Is that a Full brog?   Bull frog

Have you seen Killy the Bid?
Billy the Kid

Play chair don't feat
Play fair don't cheat

The sip shailed   ship sailed

She has hig bipps   big hips

"Oh see can you say"
"Oh say can you see"

PRO   TEAMS

Bicago Chulls	Chicago Bulls
Diami Molphins	Miami Dolphins
Ros Angeles Lams	Los Angeles Rams
Rashington Wedskins	Washington Redskins
Letroit Dions	Detroit Lions
Callas Dowboys	Dallas Cowboys
Eiladelphia Peasgles	Philidelphia Eagles

News Headlines

Pinton Incleached
Clinton Impeached

Pixon imneached
Nixon impeached

Will Prump be imtreached
Will Trump be impeached

Should DUTIN PISAPPEAR

Should PUTIN   DISAPPEAR

CITIES

Salm Prings   Palm Spring

Vula Chista, CA   Chula Vista, CA

Manta Sonica, CA   Santa Monica, CA

Rand Grapids, MI   Grand Rapids, MI

Wort Forth, TX   Fort Worth, Texas

Tallas. Dexas   Dallas, TX

Caaadena, PA   Pasadena, CA.

BonLong Beach, CA. Long Beach, CA

Heverly Bills, CA   Beverly Hills, CA

Horth Nollywood   North Hollywood, CA

Bouth Send   South Bend, IN

I MET A LOT OF
Famous People While opening
new Restaurants
Airport Food and Beverage
Facilities and In - Flight
Food and Beverage Services

`Nayne Wewton
Wayne Newton

Noe Jamath
Joe Namath

Lerry Jewis
Jerry Lewis

Bona Rerrett
Rona Berrett

Mean Dartin
Dean Martin

Gobert Roulet
Robert Goulet

Hob Bope   **Bob Hope**

Cobert Rulp   **Robert Culp**

Dammy Savis   **Sammy Davis jr.**

Gary Crant
Cary Grant

Pegory Greck
Gregory Peck

Huddy Backet
Buddy Hacket

Sank Frinatra
Frank Sinatra

Billy Kilmer
Killy Bilmrt

Bumphrey Hogart
Humphrey Bogart

Pane Jowell
Jane Powell

Jan Vohnson
Van Johnson

Barles Chronso
Charles Bronson

Hita Rayworth
Rita Hayworth

Lart Inkletter
Art Linkletter

hmmmm???
Doris Day

hmmmm???
Dianna Dors

Von Joight
Jon Voight

Tel Morme
Mel Torme

Dimmy Jurante
Jimmy Durante

Chyd Chari
Cyd Charis

Polly Dorton
Dolly Parton

Mony Tartin   Tony Martin

Rane Jussell
Jane Russell

Croderic Brawford
Broderic Crawford

Chulie Jristy
July Christy

Raesar Comero
Caesar Romero

Coan Jollins
Joan Collins

Bedd Eyrnes
Edd Byrnes

Arbara Beden   Barbara Eden

Bes Lrown   Les Brown

Terley Shempl   Shirley Temple

Ronald Reagan
Met Ron and family at
Diamond Jim's Restaurant
Hollywood

Rebbie Deynolds
Debbie Reynolds

Conald O Donner
Donald O Conner

Waquel Relch
Raquel Welch

Stonnie Cevens   Connie Stevens

Mann Niller
Ann Miller

Cony Turtis
Tony Curtis

hmmmm??
Susan Summers

Lanet Jiegh
Janet Liegh

Mee Lajors
Lee Majors

Sichard Rimmons
Richard Simmons

Mee Larvin
Lee Marvin

Beorge Gurns
George Burns

Iohn Jreland
John Ireland

Wack Jebb
Jack Webb

Mictor Vature
Victor Mature

Spark Mitz
Mark Spitz

Werry Jest
Jerry West

Eyatt Warp   Wyatt Earp

Natum O Teal
Tatum O Neal

Nyan O Real
Ryan O Neal

Chilt Wamberlin
Wilt Chamberlin

Cerry Pomo
Perry Como

Gancho Ponzales
Poncho Gonzales

Mayton Cloore   Clayton Moore

Wester Eilliams
Ester Williams

Jon Dohnson   Don Johnson

Gohn Jilbert
John Gilbert

Cathy Krosby
Kathy Crosby

Tree Levino
Lee Trevino

Crob Bosby   Bob Crosby

Bat Putrum   Pat Butrum

Aob Babernathy
Bob Abernathy

Bedgar Euchanan
Edgar Buchanan

Oy Traikman
Troy Aikman

Dodney Rangerfield
Rodney Dangerfield

Fret Barve
Bret Farve

Wack Jorden
Jack Warden

Cick Dantino
Dick Cantino

Bonny Sono
Sonny Bono

Chrinda Listian
Linda Christian

`Wale Yexler
Yale Wexler

Red Buttons   Red Buttons

Gohnny Jrant
Johnny Grant

Whessie Jite
Jessie White

Berry Tradshaw
Terry Bradshaw

Back Jenny.
Jack Benny

Brell Mooks   Mel Brooks

Mennis the Denace
Dennis the Menace

Tiz Laylor   Liz Taylor

hmmmm??
Susan Serandon

Bat Poone   Pat Boone

Cary Gooper
Gary Cooper

Bobby Berman
Bobby Sherman

Huddy Backet   Buddy Hacket

Lavey Dopes
Davey Lopes

Kan Stenton
Stan Kenton

Shearl Ieb
Earl Sheib

Hustin Doffman
Dustin Hoffman

Reorge Gaft
George Raft

O.J. Simpson
So.J. Impson

Wohnny Jeismiller
Johnny Weismiller

Green Joe Mean
Mean Joe Green

Wob Baterfield
Bob Waterfield

On Jarnett
Jon Arnett

Grorne Leen
Lorne Green

Ichard Randerson
Richard Anderson

Dince Vedrick
Vince Dedrick
Vince was Lee Majors Stand in for films and TV
and my neighbor

hmmm??
Corrine Calvet

Ran Dather   Dan Rather

.

Dam Sonaldson
Sam Donaldson

Garley Chibson
Charley Gibson

Bom Trokaw   Tom Brokaw

Lush Rimbaugh
Rush Limbaugh

Loan Jundon   Joan Lundon

Cill Blinton
Bill Clinton

Cllary Hinton
Hillary Clinton

Milly Ways   **Willy Mays**

Man Stuial
Stan Musial

Vobby Binton
Bobby Vinton

Coseph Jotten
Joseph Cotten

Clint Eastwood
East Clintwood

Dill Bana   **Bill Dana**

Dob Bole
Bob Dole

Games Jarner
James Garner

Kani Lazan
Lani Kazan

Ham Sanks   Sam Hanks

Cou Lostello
Lou Costello

Myvette Imieux
Yvette Mimieux

Beorge Gush   George Bush

Nichard Rixon
Richard Nixon

Beorge Glanda
George Blanda

Wohn Jooden
John Wooden

hmmmm??
Farah Faucett

Poodle dage

Think about and make notes or add thoughts

on the Doodle Page

FRIENDS WHILE GROWING UP

Wen Gunderwood Gwen Underwood

Bale Danta   Dale Banta

Dilly Bick   Billy Dick

Pusan Sratt   Susan Pratt

Birginia Vonville   Virginia Bonville

Moris BcClain   Doris McClain

Gean Joz   Jean Goz

Peslie Lerlmutter   Leslie Perlmutter

Thonny Rorman	Ronny Thorman
Ped Eterson	Ed Peterson
Eill Bedwards	Bill Edwards
Mommy Tinor	Tommy Minor

ASTRONAUTS
Apollo VII

Eon   Disle   **Don Eisle**

Shally Wirra   **Wally Shirra**

Calter Wunningham

Walter Cunningham

Walt was My high school buddy
Venice Hi School 1950   California

1968

To PATTI & TOM,
Come fly with
me on APOLLO VII,

Walt

WALLY SHIRRA   WALT CUNNINHAM   DONN EISLE

Rubber Bumpers now being manufactured for child miniature driven race cars.

Just what I am looking for
BUBBER   RUMPERS

For all you laseball bovers

they are warming up

in a pull ben.

The game is on, he just thole stird,

the runner was plown out at the thrate.

Open the door Richard

Open the door Richard

Richard why won't you

Open the door and let me in.

GIZZA and PRILL

Really FOOD GOOD

Poodle dage

Think about and make notes or add thoughts

on the Doodle Page

Standin on the corner watchin

all the girls go by.

It could all be over,

by   a bild wullet

or a bray stullet

could take it all away

The wind blew
eirt in my dyes

dirt in my eyes

My rear hit the dirt first
when my cike brashed

bike crashed

I am heading to bail

cause I can't find jail

I am heading to jail

cause I can't find bail

Certificate of Registration

This Certificate issued under the seal of the Copyri
Office in accordance with title 17, *United States Coc*
attests that registration has been made for the worl
identified below. The information on this certificat
been made a part of the Copyright Office records.

Shira Perlmutter

United States Register of Copyrights and Director

Title

Title of Work: Spoonerism & The Backassv

Completion/Publication

Year of Completion: 2020

Author

Author: Thomas Fallin Wagner
Author Created: text, photograph(s)
Work made for hire: No
Citizen of: United States
Year Born: 1931
Anonymous: No
Pseudonymous: No

Copyright Claimant

That's all folks!!!!!